SpringerBriefs in Health Care Management and Economics

Series Editor
Joseph K. Tan, McMaster University, Burlington, ON, Canada

W0234447

For further volumes:
http://www.springer.com/series/10293

Maartje E. Zonderland

Appointment Planning
in Outpatient Clinics
and Diagnostic Facilities

 Springer

Maartje E. Zonderland
Zonderland Healthcare Logistics
Laag-Soeren, The Netherlands

ISSN 2193-1704   ISSN 2193-1712 (electronic)
ISBN 978-1-4899-7450-1   ISBN 978-1-4899-7451-8 (eBook)
DOI 10.1007/978-1-4899-7451-8
Springer New York Heidelberg Dordrecht London

Library of Congress Control Number: 2014936199

Printed on acid-free paper

Springer is part of Springer Science+Business Media (www.springer.com)

Preface

This monograph aims to provide a concise overview of various aspects of appointment planning in healthcare, more specific in outpatient clinics and diagnostic facilities. The reader is provided with a basic overview of relevant mathematical models and simple queuing theory calculations that support the development and improvement of appointment systems. Access time and waiting list management is discussed, followed by guidelines for scheduling of appointment slots, specific appointment systems, and a set of rules that help the reader to improve clinic operations. The last chapter discusses future challenges related to the topic. This monograph is written for both operations research professionals with an interest in healthcare and healthcare professionals with an interest in appointment planning.

Laag-Soeren, The Netherlands   Maartje E. Zonderland

Contents

Chapter 1
Introduction

This chapter introduces relevant concepts and themes, related to appointment planning in healthcare, with a focus on outpatient clinics and diagnostic facilities.

1.1 Typical Outpatient Clinics and Diagnostic Facilities

The most important feature of an outpatient clinic (or ambulatory care facility) is that it provides care in an ambulatory care setting. This basically means that patients follow the route *Home → Outpatient clinic → Home*.

Outpatient clinics are usually organized around a single specialty (Gynecology, Ophthalmology, etc.) or around a certain disease or symptoms (for example, sleeping disorders). In the latter case these clinics are usually multidisciplinary, which means that several specialties are involved. Common activities carried out at outpatient clinics are intakes, treatment and follow-up of patients. Simple diagnostic activities such as blood withdrawal or performing ECG tests are often also planned here.

The term "outpatient clinic" is diffuse; sometimes, it is used to refer to an entire, physical clinic. For example: "the Gynecology and Urology outpatient clinic is situated in building A and opens every day from 8AM-5PM". In other cases it is used to refer to a specific time interval in which one or more medical professionals are planned for consultations, sometimes even for a specific disease. For example: "doctor B, Urologist, is available for consultations regarding prostate cancer each Tuesday and Friday from 1–5PM." In this monograph, the term "outpatient clinic" refers to both entities. With the mathematical tools provided it is possible to develop appointment systems for the entire clinic or only a part of it (i.e., for a specific physician, a specific day, and so on).

At diagnostic facilities, and some outpatient clinics, not only outpatients but also inpatients (patients currently admitted in the hospital) and patients from the emergency department (ED) are examined. In the case of outpatient clinics this usually involves inpatients requiring a minor procedure which cannot be carried out at

M.E. Zonderland, *Appointment Planning in Outpatient Clinics and Diagnostic Facilities*, SpringerBriefs in Health Care Management and Economics, DOI 10.1007/978-1-4899-7451-8_1, © The Author 2014

the nursing ward. Diagnostic tests are usually performed at a centralized diagnostic facility; only large EDs have their own diagnostic equipment. Examples of diagnostic tests are X-rays, magnetic resonance imaging (MRI scan), computed tomography (CT scan), and position emission tomography (PET scan). The time required to perform a diagnostic test varies from very short (X-ray; usually 5–10 min including positioning of the patient) to quite long (MRI scans can easily take up to 1.5 h). Skilled staff is required to operate the equipment.

The planning of diagnostic tests is usually quite involved; this is related to the availability and skills of staff (technicians can operate only a limited number of machine types), variations in patient demand, patient mix and arrival patterns, variation in duration of the tests, switch-over times if a different type of test is planned on the machine, and cohesion with care processes at other hospital departments (for instance, when the MRI scan is part of a care pathway organized around a certain type of disease or patient). An additional complicating factor in academic hospitals is the usage of equipment for research activities.

1.2 Patient Types

Two different patient type classifications are introduced. The first classification is based on urgency, the second on admission status.

1.2.1 Patient Classification Based on Urgency

Roughly, three different patient types can be distinguished when patients are classified using urgency as a criterion. The first type regards elective patients; for these patients their treatment or consultation can be planned some time in advance. The second type considers urgent patients. These patients cannot be planned in advance and require immediate care upon arrival at the hospital, where the majority of urgent patients enter the hospital through the ED. The third type includes patients who cannot be included in either the elective or the urgent category. These patients are given the semi-urgent (or semi-elective) status. The exact definition of this patient type may vary per country, hospital, and even hospital department, but in general these patients do not require immediate treatment upon arrival, but do require treatment within a certain amount of time, for instance within a day, a week, or 2 weeks. Most elective patients will ultimately evolve into semi-urgent or even urgent patients if treatment is extensively prolonged.

1.2.2 Patient Classification Based on Admission Status

As mentioned earlier, outpatients usually follow the route *Home → Outpatient clinic → Home*. Inpatients are admitted at a nursing ward, their admission including at least one overnight stay. However, this, historically, clear distinction between in- and outpatients is not so evident anymore. Lately, a shift from inpatient to outpatient care has been emerging, where an increased number of patients are treated in an outpatient setting. Even surgical procedures for which extensive hospitalization was required in the past are now performed in so-called Short Stay Units, where the entire admission, treatment, and discharge process are planned on a single day. Also, mixed forms of in- and outpatient care are evolving, for example in which the patient is treated at an outpatient clinic for two consecutive days and stays overnight in a "care hotel." Thus, whether a patient is classified as an in- or an outpatient is also a managerial decision. An additional entrance route is through the emergency department. These patients are, at the start of their care trajectory, usually referred to as emergency patients. Once they are admitted at a regular ward, they become inpatients.

1.3 Planning Types

Patients can be planned for a single consultation, treatment, or test in two ways: they can be given an appointment or enter the clinic within a pre-specified time frame whenever they want. The latter is referred to as "walk-in." An appointment basically states the date and time the patient is expected. Usually a time slot is reserved for the patient, although it is not uncommon to reserve a single time slot for multiple patients. This is called over-booking.

Since appointments can be planned by the clinic, the clinic has maximal influence on the distribution of patient arrivals over the day and day of the week. If an appointment system is well organized, patients receive treatment shortly after arrival and the care provider's work pressure is more or less constant. However, we probably all know many examples of clinics where this is not the case.

In a walk-in clinic, the patients arrive ad hoc, or randomly. The advantage of this is that patients can, to a great extent, decide when they visit the clinic. Also, they can combine this visit with visits to other hospital departments. A huge disadvantage of patients walking in, however, is that the usually strong fluctuating arrival stream can result in an overcrowded clinic, leading to long waiting times, high peaks in care provider's working pressure, and patients leaving without treatment (blocking). On other moments of time the waiting room will be practically empty. These issues will be discussed extensively in Chaps. 5 and 7, together with tips and tricks to organize a walk-in clinic such that waiting times and blocking are reduced and the care provider's working pressure is leveled.

1.4 Two Important Concepts: Access and Waiting Time

Next to the medical aspects of the treatment, two concepts are of interest for patients: access time and waiting time. Access time refers to the time interval between the appointment request and the day of the actual appointment. Access time is usually measured in days, or even weeks, and is closely related to waiting lists. If the waiting list contains 80 patients who are treated on order of arrival, and each week 8 patients are treated, then the access time is 10 weeks (80 patients divided by 8 patients per week).

Waiting time is defined as the time the patient spends at the clinic before the treatment, consultation, or test starts. It is usually measured in minutes or even hours. Suppose the appointment is scheduled to start at 10 a.m., and actually starts at 10:15 a.m., then the waiting time is 15 min. It is not uncommon that patients arrive too early for their appointment. This extra time is usually not considered as waiting time by clinic management; however, it can be perceived as such by patients. See also Fig. 1.1.

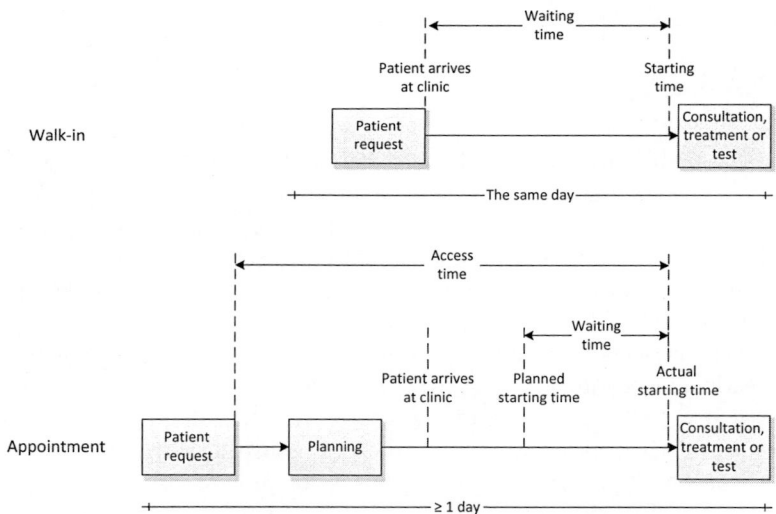

Fig. 1.1 Access and waiting time

1.5 Common Appointment Systems

Most appointment systems are quite simple. First a time frame is defined in which the appointments should be planned (for instance, 9 a.m.–1 p.m.). Then the time interval (4 h in this case) is divided into slots of equal length, usually 5, 10, 15, 20, or 30 min. The usage of 5-min multiples is motivated by psychological and technical factors. In most appointment planning software only appointment slots with a length which is a multiple of 5 min can be defined. Also, for both patients, administrative and medical staff it is hard to work with appointments which are, for instance, 12 or 18 min.

After defining the slot length, patient types are specified. Next to the classifications based on urgency and admission status, additional criteria such as "new patient" or "check-up" are used. Sometimes multiple patients are planned for the first slot, so that the risk of idle time (time the care provider is waiting for patients to arrive) is minimized. This originates from the famous Bailey–Welch rule [1], developed already in 1952. For some patient types double slots are booked. It is quite common to block time slots for specific patient types, especially at diagnostic facilities. However, this introduces a lot of inflexibility and should be avoided as much as possible (this will be discussed in Chaps. 5 and 7).

1.6 Hierarchical Decision Making

Day-to-day patient planning involves operational decisions. All other decisions mentioned in the previous paragraph are tactical. The strategical decisions (see [2] for a discussion of planning and control in healthcare) that should precede the tactical and operational level are often neglected. Next to the weeks and days of operation and the opening hours, clinic and hospital management should also consider the distribution of patients over medical specialties and individual care providers. Furthermore, the distribution of physical space over specialties and individual care providers should be subject of discussion and not be based on historical privileges (see also [3] for a discussion on planning and control decisions in ambulatory care facilities). Also, on a meta level the distribution of patients over hospitals and hospital locations is becoming more and more a point of discussion. From a financial, societal, and medical perspective it is simply not acceptable anymore to provide a complete supply of care in each hospital.

Figure 1.2 shows an example of decisions, from a strategical to a tactical and operational level, to consider during the development of an appointment system. Important performance measures that should influence these decisions are patient access and waiting time, and care providers idle time and work pressure. In the remainder of this book we show how mathematical modeling can support the development of appointment systems (Chaps. 2 and 3). We also provide practical guidelines related to access time and waiting list management (Chap. 4), scheduling of appointment slots (Chap. 5), specific appointment systems such as advanced access and walk-in (Chap. 6), and the improvement of clinic operations (Chap. 7). Chapters 2 and 3 provide mathematical theory to support the topics discussed in later chapters. The reader may choose to omit these chapters and use them, if desired, at a later point for reference.

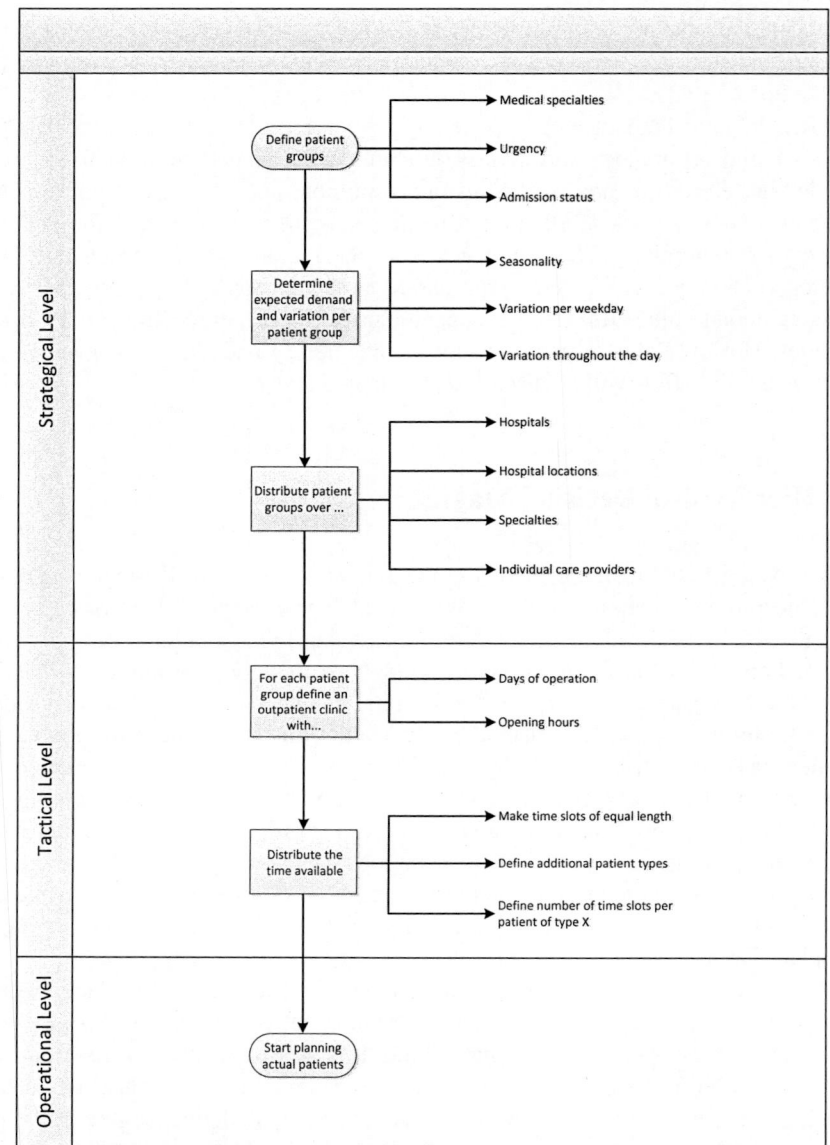

Fig. 1.2 Roadmap for appointment systems design

References

[1] Bailey NTJ (1952) A study of queues and appointment systems in hospital out-patient departments, with special reference to waiting-times. J R Stat Soc Ser B Stat Methodol 14(2):185–199

[2] Hans EW, van Houdenhoven M, Hulshof PJH (2012) A framework for healthcare planning and control. In: Hall RW (eds) Handbook of healthcare system scheduling. Springer, New York

[3] Hulshof PJH, Kortbeek N, Boucherie RJ, Hans EW, Bakker PJM (2012) Taxonomic classification of planning decisions in healthcare: a structured review of the state of the art in OR/MS. Health Syst 1(2):129–175

Chapter 2
Mathematical Models for Appointment Planning

Up to date, a vast amount of theoretical work has evolved around the subject of appointment planning, where the majority of literature appeared in the last 10–15 years. It goes beyond the scope of this book to provide a complete overview, especially since there are already several excellent review articles available. The studies in [2, 5, 7] provide good starting points for those interested. In this chapter we use the taxonomy as defined in [7] to provide a brief introduction to the most commonly used mathematical models in appointment planning. The taxonomy classifies literature on outpatient clinics, or ambulatory care services, using a two-dimensional system. The first dimension involves the planning decision and the hierarchical level in the decision-making process: strategic, tactical, offline operational, and online operational. All steps from the roadmap introduced in Chap. 1 of this book (Fig. 1.2) are considered, together with additional decisions such as facility layout, patient routing, staff-shift scheduling, and staff-to-shift assignment.

The second dimension of the taxonomy in [7] considers the mathematical method used. In the next sections we discuss three mathematical modeling methods: computer simulation, Markov decision processes, and queuing theory. All these methods have stochastic elements. This means that uncertainty is taken into account by introducing random variables. A random variable has a set of possible values, each associated with a certain probability. For example, the outcome of rolling a dice is a random variable with possible outcomes 1–6, each with probability $\frac{1}{6}$. In a health-care setting, the number of patients calling for an appointment on Monday can be modeled using a random variable, just as the length of a consultation. Due to the high variability that is usually observed in healthcare settings, introducing stochasticity in the modeling process is very important to obtain valuable and reasonable results.

M.E. Zonderland, *Appointment Planning in Outpatient Clinics and Diagnostic Facilities*, SpringerBriefs in Health Care Management and Economics, DOI 10.1007/978-1-4899-7451-8_2, © The Author 2014

2.1 Computer Simulation

Computer simulation, or simulation, is a widely used approach to study healthcare problems (see, e.g., the review articles [1, 8]; see [10, 12] for a generic introduction to simulation). The system which is studied is represented by developing a simulation model. Probability distributions and/or random number generators are used to mimic the behavior of key elements in the system. Not only commercial but also open source simulation software packages allow the modeler to carry out numerical experiments where the system's behavior is simulated over a certain period of time. Due to the stochastic elements introduced by the probability distributions and random numbers, the system's behavior will be different for each experiment, even though the input variables are the same. Results are obtained by computing a large number of experiments and then calculating the average values and standard deviations of the outcome variables.

Simulation allows for extensive scenario analysis, although the inclusion of various scenarios in the software can be very time consuming. It is, however, a very valuable tool since it allows the modeler to make a representation of the problem which is very close to reality. This is at the same time one of the major drawbacks of simulation; since almost anything can be modeled, it is very tempting to do so. As a result, sometimes the focus moves from making a thorough analysis of a problem to making a good as possible representation of the problem in the simulation software. Another drawback is that usually a large amount of data and computation time is required [4]. With regard to appointment planning, simulation is typically used to evaluate appointment schedules (see, e.g., [3, 6]).

2.2 Markov Decision Processes

A Markov decision process (see [11] for an introduction) can be used to model a system where (it can be assumed that) events which occurred in the past (i.e., before the system reached the current state) do not influence the sequence of events in the future: the so-called Markov property. Therefore, Markov processes are commonly used to model systems where the state of the system partially or completely depends on chance. The main goal of a Markov decision model is to determine an optimal policy for a given problem, for instance the number of semi-urgent surgeries to schedule this week, given the expected demand for semi-urgent surgeries next week [14], or the number of appointment patients to schedule given the expected demand of walk-in patients [9]. In both cases it is assumed the number of this week's patient arrivals is not influenced by the number of patients who arrived last week (so the Markov property is satisfied). Note that the formulation of a Markov model requires in-depth mathematical knowledge.

2.3 Queuing Theory

Queuing theory (see [13] for an introduction) is a common tool to analyze waiting times and service levels in service systems. It is, for example, used to determine the number of operators in call centers, given certain performance measures such as the number of incoming calls that have to wait. A queuing model in a health-care setting usually consists of patient arrival and service processes, the number of servers (for instance, the number of doctors working at an outpatient clinic), and the service discipline (for example, first come, first serve; see Chap. 3 for an explanation of the aforementioned concepts). Simple queuing models are easy to analyze; however, for state-of-the-art queuing models, as well as with Markov decision processes, advanced mathematical skills are required. This especially involves non-steady state analysis (in this type of queuing models it is not assumed, as opposed to other (steady state) queuing models, that the service and arrival processes are homogeneous in time). A queuing model can be time consuming to formulate, but subsequently scenario and bottleneck analysis can be performed quite fast and easy.

2.4 Wrap-up

Many work has been done on appointment planning in healthcare. However, there is still a large gap between theory and practice. Often, researchers solve a fictitious problem instead of a real-world problem from a healthcare organization. Even if a real problem is used it is sometimes unclear whether the solution has been implemented, and even more important, if it worked. This is related to several issues. First of all, the people in the hospitals experiencing the problem (in this case appointment planners, doctors, outpatient clinic secretaries, and so on) usually do not have access to operations research specialists. Second, operations research specialists working at universities often do not have access to healthcare organizations. Fortunately, several initiatives and operations research in healthcare groups have evolved over the last decade worldwide. But there is still a long way to go. Implementation of change and different working routines can, as in many other industries, be very challenging in healthcare, and deserves more attention.

One of the aims of this book is to provide a set of tools to improve appointment planning. All three methods explained in this chapter require a certain amount of mathematical knowledge and modeling time. However, queuing theory also provides possibilities for simple, hand-on analysis of important questions that come across in appointment planning. Therefore the next chapter introduces basic queuing theory concepts, followed by Chaps. 4–7 which describe these possibilities.

References

[1] Brailsford SC, Harper PR, Patel B, Pitt M (2009) An analysis of the academic literature on simulation and modelling in health care. J Simul 3:130–140

[2] Cayirli T, Veral E (2003) Outpatient scheduling in health care: a review of literature. Prod Oper Manag 12(4):519–549

[3] Cayirli T, Veral E, Rosen H (2006) Designing appointment scheduling systems for ambulatory care services. Health Care Manag Sci 9(1):47–58

[4] Cochran JK, Roche KT (2009) A multi-class queuing network analysis methodology for improving hospital emergency department performance. Comput Oper Res 36(5):1497–1512

[5] Gupta D, Denton B (2008) Appointment scheduling in health care: challenges and opportunities. IIE Trans 40(9):800–819

[6] Harper PR, Gamlin HM (2003) Reduced outpatient waiting times with improved appointment scheduling: a simulation modelling approach. OR Spectr 25(2):207–222

[7] Hulshof PJH, Kortbeek N, Boucherie RJ, Hans EW, Bakker PJM (2012) Taxonomic classification of planning decisions in healthcare: a structured review of the state of the art in OR/MS. Health Syst 1(2):129–175

[8] Jun JB, Jacobson SH, Swisher JR (1999) Application of discrete-event simulation in healthcare: a survey. J Oper Res Soc 50(2):109–123

[9] Kortbeek N, Zonderland ME, Braaksma A, Vliegen IMH, Boucherie RJ, Litvak N, Hans EW (2011) Designing cyclic appointment schedules for outpatient clinics with scheduled and unscheduled patient arrivals. Memorandum 1968, Department of Applied Mathematics, University of Twente, Enschede, The Netherlands

[10] Law AM, Kelton WD (1991) Simulation modeling and analysis. McGraw-Hill, New York

[11] Puterman ML (1994) Markov decision processes: discrete stochastic dynamic programming. Wiley, New York

[12] Winston WL (1994) Operations research: applications and algorithms, 3rd edn. Duxbury Press, Belmont

[13] Wolff RW (1989) Stochastic modeling and the theory of queues. Prentice Hall, Englewood Cliffs

[14] Zonderland ME, Boucherie RJ, Litvak N, Vleggeert-Lankamp CLAM (2010) Planning and scheduling of semi-urgent surgeries. Health Care Manag Sci 13(3):256–267

Chapter 3
Basic Queuing Theory

In this chapter we introduce basic elements from queuing theory. This chapter is written for those with a deeper (theoretical) interest in queuing theory. The reader can also skip this part and use it for reference purposes only. The majority of the text in this chapter appeared previously in [13].

3.1 Some General Queuing Concepts

A queue can generally be characterized by its arrival and service processes, the number of servers, and the service discipline (Fig. 3.1). The arrival process is specified by a probability distribution that has an arrival rate associated with it, which is usually the mean number of patients who arrives during a time unit (e.g., minutes, hours, or days). A common choice for the probabilistic arrival process is the Poisson process, in which the inter-arrival times of patients are independent and exponentially distributed.

The service process specifies the service requirements of patients, again using a probability distribution with associated service rate. A common choice is the exponential distribution, which is convenient for obtaining analytical tractable results. The number of servers in a healthcare setting may represent the number of doctors at an outpatient clinic, the number of MRI scanners at a diagnostic department, and so on. The service discipline specifies how incoming patients are served. The most common discipline is first come first serve (FCFS), where patients are served in order of arrival. Some patients may have priority over other patients. This can be such that the service of a lower priority patient is interrupted when a higher priority patient arrives (preemptive priority), or the service of the lower priority patient is finished first (non-preemptive priority).

M.E. Zonderland, *Appointment Planning in Outpatient Clinics and Diagnostic Facilities*, SpringerBriefs in Health Care Management and Economics, DOI 10.1007/978-1-4899-7451-8_3, © The Author 2014

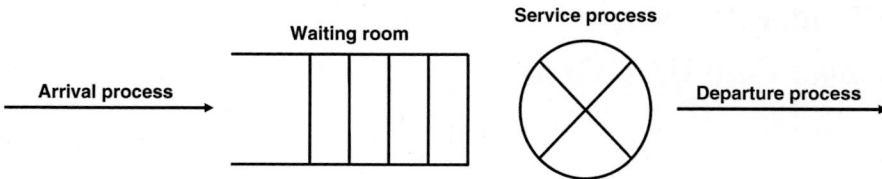

Fig. 3.1 A simple queue

3.1.1 Performance Measures

Typical measures for the performance of a system include the mean sojourn time, $\mathbb{E}[W]$, the mean time that a patient spends in the queue and in service. The sojourn time is a random variable as it is determined by the stochastic arrival and service processes. The mean waiting time, $\mathbb{E}[W^q]$, gives the mean time a patient spends in the queue waiting for service. How $\mathbb{E}[W]$ and $\mathbb{E}[W^q]$ are calculated depends, among other things, on the choice for the arrival and service processes, and is given for several basic queues in Sect. 3.2.

Kendall's Notation

All queues in this book are described using the so-called Kendall notation: $A/B/s$, where **A** denotes the arrival process, **B** denotes the service process, and **s** is the number of servers. There are several extensions to this notation, see, for example, [10]. Clearly, there are many distinctive cases of queues:

$M/M/1$: The single-server queue with Poisson arrivals and exponential service times. The M stands for the *M*arkovian or *M*emoryless property.
$M/D/1$: The single-server queue with Poisson arrivals and *D*eterministic service times.
$M/G/1$: The single-server queue with Poisson arrivals and *G*eneral (i.e., not specified) service time distribution.

Other arrival processes may also apply: consider, for example, the $D/M/1$, $G/M/1$ and $G/G/1$ queue. All of the forms above also exist in the case of multiple servers ($s > 1$).

3.1.2 Load

The load of the queue is defined as the mean utilization rate per server, which is the amount of work that arrives on average per time unit, divided by the amount of work the queue can handle on average per time unit. Suppose our server is a single doctor in an outpatient clinic, then the load specifies the fraction of time the doctor is working. More specifically, the load, ρ, equals the amount of work brought to the system per time unit, i.e. the patient arrival rate, λ, multiplied by the mean service time per patient, $\mathbb{E}[S]$:

$$\rho = \lambda \mathbb{E}[S]. \tag{3.1}$$

The load is the fraction of time the server, working at unit rate, must work to handle the arriving amount of work. It is required that $\rho < 1$ (in other words, the server should work less than 100 % of the time). If $\rho > 1$, then on average more work arrives at the queue than can be handled, which inevitably leads to a continuously growing number of patients in the queue waiting for service, i.e., an unstable system. Only when the arrival and service processes are deterministic (i.e., the inter-arrival and service times have zero variance), the load may equal 1.

3.1.3 Relationship Between Mean Waiting Time and Load

The mean waiting time, $\mathbb{E}[W^q]$, increases with load ρ. As an illustration, consider a single-server queue with Poisson arrivals and general service times (the so-called $M/G/1$ queue), with mean $\mathbb{E}[S]$ and squared coefficient of variation (scv) c_S^2, which is calculated by dividing the variance by the squared mean. For this queue, the relationship between ρ and $\mathbb{E}[W^q]$ is characterized by the Pollaczek–Khinchine formula [1]:

$$\mathbb{E}[W^q] = \mathbb{E}[S] \frac{\rho}{1-\rho} \frac{1+c_S^2}{2}, \tag{3.2}$$

In Fig. 3.2 the relation is shown graphically for $c_S^2 = 1$. We see that the mean waiting time increases with the load. When the load is low, a small increase therein has a minimal effect on the mean waiting time. However, when the load is high, a small increase has a tremendous effect on the mean waiting time. For instance, note that increasing the load from 50 to 55 % increases the waiting time by 10 %, but increasing the load from 90 to 95 % increases the waiting time by 100 %! This explains why a minor change (for example, a small increase in the number of patients, a patient arriving in a bed or a wheelchair) can result in a major increase in waiting times as sometimes seen in outpatient clinics.

Formulas such as (3.2) allow for an exact and fast quantification of the relationships between (influenceable) parameters and system outcomes. Queuing theory is a very valuable tool to identify bottlenecks and to calculate the effect of removing them.

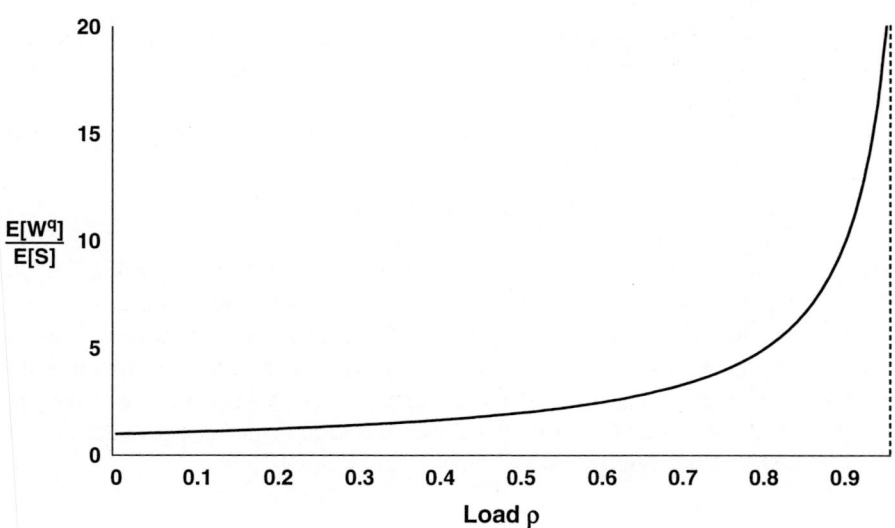

Fig. 3.2 The relationship between load ρ and mean waiting time $\mathbb{E}[W^q]$ for the $M/M/1$ queue with Poisson arrivals and exponential service times

3.1.4 The Poisson Process

As mentioned before, the Poisson process is commonly used to model the arrival of customers to a queue and in general to model independent arrivals from a large population. As an example, consider patient arrivals at a hospital emergency department (ED). They originate from a large population (the demographic area surrounding the hospital) and usually arrive independently. The probability that an arbitrary person has an urgent medical problem is very small. Then it can be shown that the arrival process tends to a Poisson process [2].

The Poisson process is common in real-world processes and has many interesting and for analysis very useful properties. For example, the number of ticks a Geiger counter records is a Poisson process. This example also indicates that merging or splitting Poisson processes independently results in Poisson processes, as this corresponds to joining two lumps of radioactive material or breaking one lump into parts. Or, for the population example, ED arrivals from a population subgroup (men, women, children, ...) are also Poisson.

For a Poisson process, the time between two successive arrivals is exponentially distributed [11]. A very important property of the exponential distribution is that it is memoryless: the probability that the inter-arrival time exceeds $u+t$ time units, given that it already has exceeded u time units, equals the probability that the inter-arrival time exceeds t time units. Mathematically, a random variable X that has an exponential distribution satisfies:

$$\mathbb{P}(X > u+t|X > u) = \mathbb{P}(X > t), \quad \forall u,t \geq 0. \tag{3.3}$$

We may also rephrase this property as: what happens in the future is independent of what happened in the past. Because of this Markovian or memoryless property, the complexity of analyzing systems with this property significantly reduces, as we show in the subsequent subsections.

3.2 Basic Queues

We now introduce the most commonly used queues: single- and multi-server queues with Poisson arrivals and exponential or general service times. Unless mentioned otherwise, we consider the FCFS service discipline and queues with infinite capacity for waiting patients.

3.2.1 The $M/M/1$ Queue

In an $M/M/1$ queue, patients arrive according to a Poisson process with rate λ and exponentially distributed service requirement with mean service time $\mathbb{E}[S]$. The service rate per unit time is $\mu = \frac{1}{\mathbb{E}[S]}$, the number of patients that would be completed per time unit when the system would continuously be serving patients. As denoted in Sect. 3.1.2, the load of the queue is $\rho = \lambda \mathbb{E}[S]$, where it is required that $\rho < 1$, that is, the amount of work brought into the queue should be less than the working speed of the server. The number of patients present in the queue at time t, i.e., those waiting in line and in service, is obtained from Markov chain analysis.

Let $N(t)$ record the number of patients in the system at time t. Then $N = (N(t), t \geq 0)$ is a Markov chain with state space $\mathbb{N}_0 = \{0, 1, 2, \ldots\}$, arrival rate λ, which is the rate at which a transition occurs from a state with n patients to a state with $n+1$ patients, and departure rate μ from state n to state $n-1$. We are interested

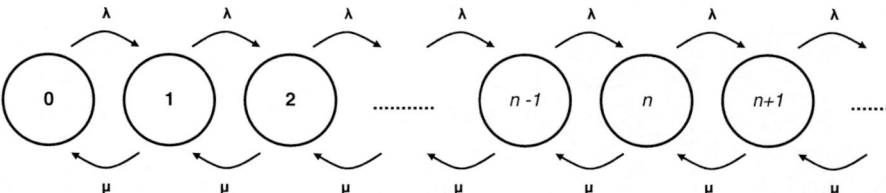

Fig. 3.3 Transition rates in the $M/M/1$ queue

in the probability P_n that at an arbitrary point in time in statistical equilibrium the system contains n patients[1]:

$$P_n = \lim_{t \to \infty} \mathbb{P}(N(t) = n). \tag{3.4}$$

The probability P_n also reflects the fraction of time that the system contains n patients. The total probability may be seen as an amount of fluid of total volume 1 that is distributed over the states of the Markov chain and flows from state to state according to the transition rates (for the $M/M/1$ queue the arrival and departure rates). The system is in statistical equilibrium when these flows out of state n balance the flows into state n for each state n, $n = 0, 1, 2, \ldots$ (see Fig. 3.3). Mathematically, this is expressed as:

$$\lambda P_0 = \mu P_1,$$
$$(\lambda + \mu)P_1 = \lambda P_0 + \mu P_2,$$
$$(\lambda + \mu)P_2 = \lambda P_1 + \mu P_3,$$
$$\vdots \tag{3.5}$$

and in general:

$$\lambda P_0 = \mu P_1,$$
$$(\lambda + \mu)P_n = \lambda P_{n-1} + \mu P_{n+1} \quad \text{for} \quad n > 0. \tag{3.6}$$

Since P_n is a probability, the summation of all probabilities P_n, $n = 0, 1, \ldots$, should equal unity:

$$\sum_{n=0}^{\infty} P_n = 1. \tag{3.7}$$

Using Eq. (3.6) and this additional property, we derive the queue length distribution P_n:

$$P_0 = 1 - \rho,$$
$$P_n = (1 - \rho)\rho^n \quad \text{for} \quad n > 0. \tag{3.8}$$

Note that P_0, also called the normalization constant, denotes the probability that there are zero patients present, but also the fraction of time the queue is empty. Further, ρ is the probability there are one or more patients present, and the fraction of time the queue is busy.

---

[1] We consider the system in statistical equilibrium only, as is customary in queuing theory. For the $M/M/1$ queue, relaxation or convergence to equilibrium usually occurs fast. See [3] for a discussion on the validity of equilibrium analysis.

The PASTA Property

In a queuing system with Poisson arrivals, the probability that an arriving patient finds n patients in the queue is equal to the fraction of time the queue contains n patients. This property is referred to as PASTA, or Poisson Arrivals See Time Averages [11].

Usually, queuing systems with non-Poisson arrival processes do not conform to this property. For example, consider the $D/D/1$ queue with deterministic inter-arrival and service times. Time is equally distributed in slots of length one, and the service time is half a slot. Suppose that at the start of each time slot a patient arrives (so the inter-arrival time is one slot). Then the queue is empty upon arrival for all patients, while half of the time the queue contains one patient.

The mean number of patients in the queue, $\mathbb{E}[L]$, including those in service, is given by:

$$\mathbb{E}[L] = \sum_{n=0}^{\infty} nP_n = \frac{\rho}{1-\rho}. \tag{3.9}$$

Since ρ is the mean utilization rate of the server, the mean number of patients waiting, $\mathbb{E}[L^q]$, equals:

$$\mathbb{E}[L^q] = \frac{\rho}{1-\rho} - \rho = \frac{\rho^2}{1-\rho}. \tag{3.10}$$

Using a basic result in queuing theory, known as Little's Law, the relationship between the mean number of patients in the queue, $\mathbb{E}[L]$, and the mean sojourn time, $\mathbb{E}[W]$, can be explicitly quantified as follows [5]:

$$\mathbb{E}[L] = \lambda\mathbb{E}[W]. \tag{3.11}$$

This also holds for the relationship between the mean number of patients waiting for service, $\mathbb{E}[L^q]$, and the mean waiting time in the queue, $\mathbb{E}[W^q]$:

$$\mathbb{E}[L^q] = \lambda\mathbb{E}[W^q]. \tag{3.12}$$

Note that the equilibrium distribution and performance measures are characterized by the single parameter ρ and can be calculated in a straightforward manner. As we will see in the subsequent subsections, this is more involved for more complicated queuing systems.

Little's Law

The simple relationship $\mathbb{E}[L] = \lambda \mathbb{E}[W]$, presented in 1961 by J.D.C. Little [5], is known as Little's Law. It relates the mean number of patients in the queue, $\mathbb{E}[L]$, the average arrival rate, λ, and the mean time the patient spends in the queue, $\mathbb{E}[W]$.

A common intuitive reasoning for obtaining Little's Law is the following. Suppose patients pay 1 Euro for each time unit they spend in the queue. On average, the queue receives $\mathbb{E}[L]$ Euro per time unit, since there are on average $\mathbb{E}[L]$ patients present in the queue. Alternatively, if each patient would pay upon entering the queue for its entire time spent in the queue, a patient would on average have to pay $\mathbb{E}[W]$ to finance the entire stay. Since each time unit on average λ patients enter the queue, the amount received by the queue per time unit then equals $\lambda \mathbb{E}[W]$. Both methods of payment must result in the same benefit for the queue, thus $\mathbb{E}[L] = \lambda \mathbb{E}[W]$. The formal proof actually follows the lines of this reasoning. It is remarkable that Little's Law requires only mild assumptions on the system in equilibrium, and is valid irrespective of the number of servers, distribution of the arrival and service processes, queuing and service order. Thus Little's Law applies to many types of queues.

3.2.2 The $M/M/s$ Queue

The $M/M/s$ queue is the multi-server variant of the $M/M/1$ queue. Patients arrive with rate λ, each patient is served by one server and a patient waits in queue when all servers are occupied. There are s servers so that the maximum service rate of the queue is $s\mu$, where μ is the service rate of the individual servers. If the number of patients in the queue, n, is less than the number of servers, s, the service rate equals $n\mu$ (see the transition rate diagram in Fig. 3.4). Again it is required that the amount of work that arrives per time unit (ρ) is less than the maximum service rate, i.e., $\rho = \lambda \mathbb{E}[S] < s$. The equilibrium distribution is obtained from:

$$\begin{aligned}
\lambda P_0 &= \mu P_1, \\
(\lambda + n\mu)P_n &= \lambda P_{n-1} + (n+1)\mu P_{n+1} \quad \text{for} \quad n < s, \\
(\lambda + s\mu)P_n &= \lambda P_{n-1} + s\mu P_{n+1} \quad \text{for} \quad n \geq s.
\end{aligned}$$

$$(3.13)$$

Thus

$$P_n = \frac{\rho^n}{m(n)} P_0, \qquad (3.14)$$

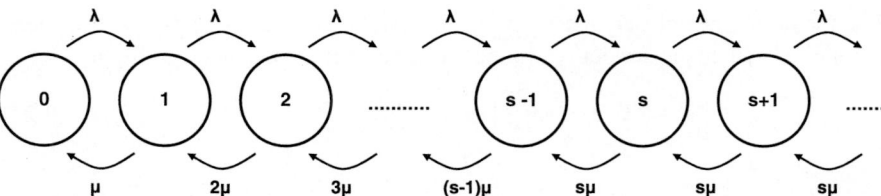

Fig. 3.4 Transition rates in the $M/M/s$ queue

where

$$m(n) = \begin{cases} n! & \text{for } 0 \leq n < s, \\ s^{n-s}s! & \text{for } n \geq s. \end{cases}$$

(3.15)

Invoking the normalization condition (3.7), we obtain:

$$P_0 = \left(\sum_{n=0}^{s-1} \frac{\rho^n}{n!} + \frac{\rho^s}{s!} \frac{s}{s-\rho} \right)^{-1}.$$

(3.16)

For $s = 1$, Eqs. (3.14)–(3.16) reduce to the queue length distribution for the $M/M/1$ queue (3.8). The probability P_s deserves special attention; this is the fraction of time all servers are occupied, and because of the PASTA property, also the fraction of arriving patients that find all servers occupied. Thus the probability that a patient will be served immediately upon arrival is $1 - \sum_{n=s}^{\infty} P_n = \sum_{n=0}^{s-1} P_n$, and the probability that a patient has to wait is $\sum_{n=s}^{\infty} P_n$. The latter probability can be calculated using the Erlang-C formula [4]:

$$P_{s+} = \mathbb{P}(n \geq s) = \frac{\rho^s}{s!} \frac{s}{s-\rho} P_0.$$

(3.17)

There are several Erlang-C calculators available online to compute P_{s+}, see, e.g., [9]. The mean number of patients waiting for service is:

$$\mathbb{E}[L^q] = \sum_{n=s+1}^{\infty} (n-s)P_n = \frac{\rho}{s-\rho} P_{s+}.$$

(3.18)

By applying Little's Law we find the mean waiting time:

$$\mathbb{E}[W^q] = \frac{\mathbb{E}[L^q]}{\lambda}.$$

(3.19)

The mean sojourn time is then obtained by adding the mean service time to the mean waiting time:

$$\mathbb{E}[W] = \mathbb{E}[S] + \mathbb{E}[W^q].$$

(3.20)

The mean number of patients in the queue can be calculated by adding the mean number of patients in service, ρ, to the mean number of patients waiting [4]:

$$\mathbb{E}[L] = \rho + \mathbb{E}[L^q]. \tag{3.21}$$

3.2.3 The $M/M/s/s$ Queue

The $M/M/s/s$ queue, or Erlang loss queue, is different from the $M/M/s$ queue in that it has no waiting capacity. Thus when all servers are occupied, patients are blocked and lost (i.e., they leave and do not come back). This type of queue is very useful when modeling healthcare systems with limited capacity, where patients are routed to another facility when all capacity is in use. Examples are nursing wards and the ICU. Figure 3.5 gives the transition rates for this queue. We obtain:

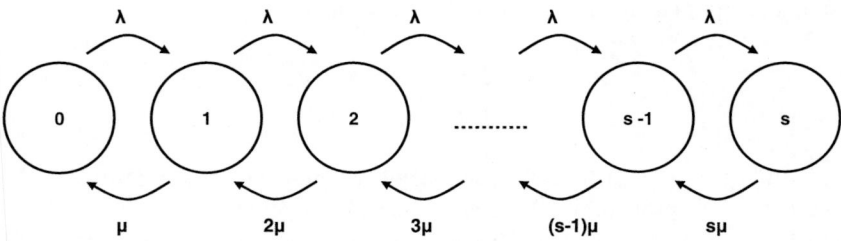

Fig. 3.5 Transition rates in the $M/M/s/s$ queue

$$\lambda P_0 = \mu P_1$$
$$(\lambda + n\mu)P_n = \lambda P_{n-1} + (n+1)\mu P_{n+1} \quad \text{for} \quad 0 < n < s$$
$$\lambda P_{s-1} = s\mu P_s, \tag{3.22}$$

with solution:

$$P_n = \frac{\rho^n/n!}{\sum_{i=0}^{s}\rho^i/i!} \quad \text{for} \quad 0 \le n \le s, \tag{3.23}$$

where $\rho = \lambda\mathbb{E}[S]$. Surprisingly, (3.23) also holds for general service times (the $M/G/s/s$ queue) and is thus insensitive to the service time distribution [4]. The probability that all servers are occupied is often called the blocking probability and is given by:

$$P_s = \frac{\rho^s/s!}{\sum_{i=0}^{s}\rho^i/i!}. \tag{3.24}$$

Formula (3.24) is often referred to as the Erlang loss formula, or Erlang-B [4]. For large s, the direct calculation of P_s by using (3.24) often introduces numerical problems. The following stable recursion exists where these problems are avoided [12].

Recursion for Erlang-B

Step 1.
Set $X_0 = 1$.

Step 2.
For $j = 1, \ldots, s$ compute

$$X_j = 1 + \frac{jX_{j-1}}{\rho}. \tag{3.25}$$

Step 3.
The blocking probability P_s is given by

$$P_s = \frac{1}{X_s}. \tag{3.26}$$

Another option is to use one of the Erlang-B calculators available online, see, e.g., [6, 9]. The performance measures are given by:

$$\mathbb{E}[L] = \rho \, (1 - P_s), \quad \mathbb{E}[W] = \mathbb{E}[S]. \tag{3.27}$$

As we have seen in this subsection, the computation of the blocking probabilities can be quite involved. The infinite server, or $M/M/\infty$ queue, is often used to approximate the $M/M/s/s$ queue for a large number of servers. In this queue, upon arrival each patient obtains his/her own server. The queue length has a Poisson distribution with parameter ρ, where $\rho = \lambda \mathbb{E}[S]$, and is thus given by

$$P_n^\infty = \frac{\rho^n}{n!} P_0, \quad \text{where}$$
$$P_0^\infty = e^{-\rho}. \tag{3.28}$$

The blocking probability for the system with s servers is approximated by Tijms [8]:

$$P_s \approx \sum_{n \geq s}^{\infty} P_n^\infty. \tag{3.29}$$

3.2.4 Queues with General Arrival and/or Service Processes

For the $M/M/s$ queue a single parameter suffices to calculate the queue length distribution and related performance measures. However, assuming exponentiality of the distributions involved in a queuing process is not always a valid choice. When the coefficient of variation is not close to 1 (the value for the exponential distribution) other probability distributions should be used to obtain reliable outcomes, since the variance of the inter-arrival and service times has strong influence on the performance measures.

Results for non-exponential systems are scarce and are often characterized via the scv, c^2. In general, when the scv increases, the variability in the related queuing system also increases. In this subsection we will focus on results for mean waiting times. Additional results are given in the books [4, 8, 11]. The software package QtsPlus that accompanies [4] supports the calculation of many relevant performance measures, is freely available online [7] and implemented in MS Excel, but also has an open source variant.

For the $M/G/1$ queue the Laplace–Stieltjes transform for the waiting time distribution is known. From this result, we obtain the Pollaczek–Khinchine formula [1] that characterizes the waiting time in the single-server queue with Poisson arrivals and general service times:

$$\mathbb{E}[W^q] = \mathbb{E}[S] \frac{\rho}{1-\rho} \frac{1+c_S^2}{2}, \tag{3.30}$$

where c_S^2 denotes the scv of the service time. The mean sojourn time for the $G/M/1$ queue is:

$$\mathbb{E}[W] = \frac{\mathbb{E}[S]}{1-\sigma}, \tag{3.31}$$

where σ is the unique root in the range $0 < \sigma < 1$ of the following equation:

$$\sigma = \bar{A}(\mu - \mu\sigma), \tag{3.32}$$

with $\bar{A}$ the Laplace–Stieltjes transform of the inter-arrival time and $\mu = \frac{1}{\mathbb{E}[S]}$ [11]. For the $G/G/1$ queue the following approximation solution is often used [8]:

$$\mathbb{E}[W^q] \approx \mathbb{E}[S] \frac{\rho}{1-\rho} \frac{c_A^2 + c_S^2}{2}, \tag{3.33}$$

where c_A^2 denotes the scv of the arrival process. This result includes the $G/M/1$ queue and is exact for the $M/G/1$ queue.

It is hard to determine the exact effect of using the exponential distribution to represent a non-exponential process. As a rule of thumb, we suggest that as long as the actual variance is below that of the exponential distribution, then the exponential distribution provides a conservative estimate. In other words, the calculated expectations of the queue length and waiting times will overestimate the actual values. Such a conservative estimate is, for instance, useful when a strategic decision that does not involve a lot of detail needs to be made.

For the mean waiting time in the $G/G/s$ queue the following approximation is very useful [4]:

$$\mathbb{E}[W^q] \approx \mathbb{E}[W_{q(M/M/s)}]\frac{c_A^2 + c_S^2}{2}, \tag{3.34}$$

where $\mathbb{E}[W_{q(M/M/s)}]$ denotes the mean waiting time in the $M/M/s$ queue with identical λ and μ. In [4] lower and upper bounds on $\mathbb{E}[W^q]$ are also provided. Using the results for $\mathbb{E}[W^q]$, Little's Law can be applied to determine the mean number of patients in the queues mentioned in this subsection.

3.3 Service Disciplines

So far, we only discussed the FCFS service discipline. Other options are processor sharing (PS) and last come first serve (LCFS). In the processor sharing service discipline, all arriving patients are immediately served, thus there is no queuing. A single server is shared equally among patients, where each patient class may have its own service requirement. For the $M/M/1 - PS$ queue the queue length distribution, P_n, is identical to that of the $M/M/1 - FCFS$ queue (3.8). Intuitively, this can be explained as follows. The server works at rate μ, and when there are n patients in the queue, an individual patient is served with rate $\frac{\mu}{n}$. However, since n patients are served simultaneously, the overall completion rate is still μ ($\frac{\mu}{n} \cdot n = \mu$). Since the patient arrival rate equals λ, the flow in and out of the queue is identical to that of the $M/M/1 - FCFS$ queue.

The $M/M/1 - LCFS$ queue with preemptive resume can be seen as a stack, for instance, of patient files, where a single server (the doctor) works on the top item of the stack. Whenever a new item is added, the server immediately starts working on this item. However, when the server returns to the previous item, it resumes service (i.e., the queue is work conserving). The queue length distribution is again given by (3.8), where the same argument holds as for the $M/M/1 - PS$ queue.

References

[1] Cohen JW (1982) The single server queue, 8th edn. North-Holland, Amsterdam
[2] de Bruin AM, Bekker R, van Zanten L, Koole GM (2010) Dimensioning hospital wards using the Erlang loss model. Ann Oper Res 178(1):23–43
[3] Green LV, Kolesar PJ, Soares J (2001) Improving the SIPP approach for staffing service systems that have cyclic demands. Oper Res 49(4):549–564
[4] Gross D, Shortle JF, Harris CM (2008) Fundamentals of queueing theory, 4th edn. Wiley, Hoboken
[5] Little JDC (1961) A proof for the queuing formula $L = \lambda W$. Oper Res 9(3):383–387

 [6] Patient Flow Improvement Center Amsterdam (2011) Erlang-B calculator. www.vumc.nl/afdelingen/pica/Software/erlang_b/. Retrieved 9 Dec 2011
 [7] QtsPlus software, available at ftp://ftp.wiley.com/public/sci_tech_med/queueing_theory/
 [8] Tijms HC (2003) A first course in stochastic models. Wiley, Chichester
 [9] Westbay Online Traffic Calculators (2011) Erlang-B calculator. www.erlang.com/calculator. Retrieved 9 Dec 2011
[10] Winston WL (1994) Operations research: applications and algorithms, 3rd edn. Duxbury Press, Belmont
[11] Wolff RW (1989) Stochastic modeling and the theory of queues. Prentice Hall, Englewood Cliffs
[12] Zeng G (2003) Two common properties of the Erlang-B function, Erlang-C function, and Engset blocking function. Math Comput Model 37(12–13):1287–1296
[13] Zonderland ME, Boucherie RJ (2012) Queuing Networks in healthcare systems. In: Hall RW (ed) Handbook of healthcare system scheduling. Springer, New York

Chapter 4
Access Time and Waiting List Management

Using the queuing theory results introduced in the previous chapter, a few simple relationships are described which provide a deeper insight in access time and waiting list management. For simplicity, weeks are chosen as time unit. This can be any other time unit, such as days, years, and hours, as long as the same time unit is used for each variable. Simple formulas originating from the $M/M/1$ queue are used in order to provide the reader with a deeper understanding of access time and waiting list management. In literature, other queuing models can be used for waiting list management as well (see, e.g., [3] where the waiting list for liver transplants is modeled using a $G/M/1$ queue). To explain the important relationship between waiting lists and facility occupation this chapter starts with the concept of occupation.

4.1 Occupation of a Resource

Using the notation introduced in Chap. 3, recall that we define λ as the number of patients calling for an appointment on average per week (e.g., patient arrivals), and μ as the number of patients that can be seen per week (e.g., the service rate). The occupation of a resource, ρ, is then given by:

$$\rho = \frac{\lambda}{\mu}. \tag{4.1}$$

This means that a fraction ρ of available capacity is used, so a fraction $1 - \rho$ of capacity is not used. To avoid unused capacity, many hospital planners and managers tend to provide an amount of capacity (i.e., appointment slots) which is equal to the average number of patients arriving each week. In this case $\rho = 1$, or 100 %. From queuing theory it is known that ρ, in case of variance in the patient arrival and/or

M.E. Zonderland, *Appointment Planning in Outpatient Clinics*
and Diagnostic Facilities, SpringerBriefs in Health Care Management and Economics,
DOI 10.1007/978-1-4899-7451-8_4, © The Author 2014

service processes,[1] should be < 1, to avoid an explosion in waiting time (see also Fig. 3.2). Figure 4.1 shows an example of the evolution of a waiting list in case $\rho = 1$. It shows clearly that the offered capacity is not sufficient if $\mu \leq \lambda$; instead,

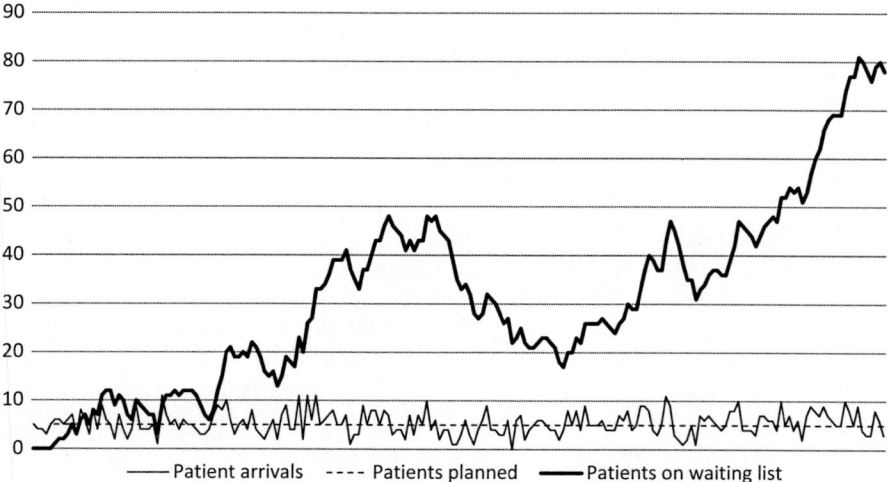

Fig. 4.1 Planning on the average number of arriving patients; evolution of the waiting list for $\lambda = \mu = 5$ ($\rho = 1$) over a period of 200 weeks, starting with an empty waiting list

$\mu > \lambda$ and thus $\rho < 1$. Figure 4.2 shows an example of the evolution of the waiting list in case $\rho = 0.83$ or 83 %. In this example the size of the waiting list is bounded; however, on average 17 % (100 − 83 %) of capacity is unused.

The challenge is to make a trade-off between maintaining a waiting list which is of acceptable size and the amount of unused capacity. Since the focus in many healthcare facilities is on avoiding unused capacity, waiting lists tend to grow until "something has to be done." Then, temporarily surplus capacity is deployed, which is usually more expensive than regular capacity, due to the usage of extra (temporarily hired) staff and working outside office hours. Even though waiting lists have a buffer function (i.e., by creating a reservoir of patients that can be planned when demand is low) it is unavoidable that, even in well-organized facilities, over a longer period of time not all capacity is used.

4.2 Access Time and Size of the Waiting List

For the $M/M/s$ queue the average access time, $\mathbb{E}[W^q]$, which is the time a patient spends on the waiting list, is given by:

---

[1] This means the number of weekly patient arrivals is not constant and/or the actual service time is not exactly the same for each patient.

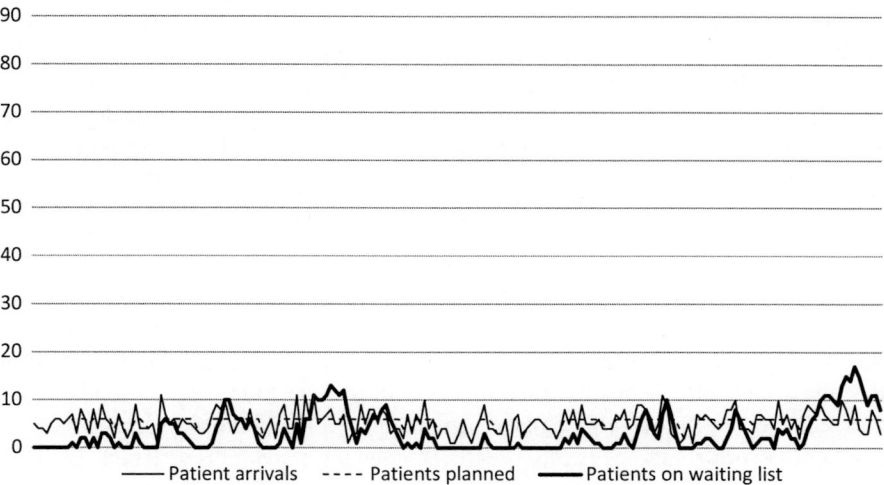

Fig. 4.2 Offering more capacity than the average number of arriving patients; evolution of the waiting list for $\lambda = 5$, $\mu = 6$ ($\rho = 0.83$) over a period of 200 weeks, starting with an empty waiting list. In this example the average access time equals 0.83 weeks, the average size of the waiting list is 4.17 patients and 17 % of capacity is unused

$$\mathbb{E}[W^q] = \frac{1}{\mu} \frac{\rho}{1-\rho} = \frac{\lambda}{\mu(\mu-\lambda)}. \tag{4.2}$$

The size of the waiting list (given in the number of patients), $\mathbb{E}[L^q]$, is calculated by multiplying the access time by the patient arrival rate, λ, and thus given by:

$$\mathbb{E}[L^q] = \lambda \mathbb{E}[W^q] = \frac{\rho^2}{1-\rho} = \frac{\lambda^2}{\mu(\mu-\lambda)}. \tag{4.3}$$

Often the maximum access time is defined. Then the number of appointments to offer per week, $\tilde{\mu}$, can be calculated using:

$$\tilde{\mu} = \left\lceil \frac{\lambda \tilde{W}^q + \sqrt{(\lambda \tilde{W}^q)^2 + 4\lambda \tilde{W}^q}}{2\tilde{W}^q} \right\rceil, \tag{4.4}$$

where $\tilde{W}^q$ represents the maximum access time and $\lceil x \rceil$ equals x rounded up to the nearest integer.

Sometimes standards are set by governmental institutions regarding the access time, such as: X % of patients should be seen within t_1 weeks, and 100 % of patients should be seen within $t_1 + t_2$ weeks. In the Netherlands, X = 80 % for regular outpatient clinic appointments, $t_1 = 3$ weeks and $t_2 = 1$ week (this is the so-called Treeknorm[2]). In practice such standards are hard to maintain and evaluate. Some patients prefer a longer access time, while for other patients a longer access time is required from a medical perspective. Whether these patients should be included in access time calculations is often unclear. Furthermore, it is notoriously difficult to

---

[2] www.treeknormen.nl.

determine the starting point of the reference period. Consider, for instance, waiting time for surgery; does it start when the patient is first seen by a doctor or when the patient is fully prepared (diagnostic testing, anesthesia check-up, and so on completed) for surgery? As a result, hospitals tend to make up their own definitions, which makes it impossible for patients to compare hospitals on meeting their access time standards.

However, a standard such as X % of patients should be seen within t_1 weeks, can be evaluated using the following formula [1]:

$$\mathbb{P}(T \le t_1) = 1 - \rho e^{-\mu(1-\rho)t_1}, \tag{4.5}$$

where e is the base of the natural logarithm and $\mathbb{P}(T \le t_1)$ represents the probability that the access time is smaller than or equal to t_1. Due to the Pasta property (see Chap. 3) the latter probability equals the percentage of patients with an access time smaller than or equal to t_1. If $\mathbb{P}(T \le t_1) \le X$, then the standard is satisfied.

Example: Suppose $t_1 = 3$ weeks, $\rho = 0.9$ and $\mu = 10$, then the fraction of patients that has an access time of at most 3 weeks equals:

$$\mathbb{P}(T \le 3) = 1 - 0.9e^{-10(1-0.9)3}$$
$$= 1 - 0.9e^{-3}$$
$$= 0.9552. \tag{4.6}$$

So in this case almost 96 % of patients has an access time of at most 3 weeks. Note that $\mathbb{P}(T \le 4) = 0.9835$, so the "100 % of patients within four weeks" requirement is not satisfied, even though a large part of patients is seen within 3 weeks.

One of the most important goals of this chapter is to show that it is impossible to use all capacity and at the same time maintain a short, manageable waiting list. A common mistake is to reason as follows:

Suppose total capacity is 100 appointments. Unused capacity is commonly used for urgent and inpatients, that can be called in last minute. 83 % of capacity is used, so there is on average 17 % of capacity available for urgent and inpatients. The urgent/inpatient demand is on average 20 apointments per day. Since 17 appointments are on average not used for elective patients, a surplus capacity of only three appointments is required to satisfy all patient demand.

Even though this is true on average, more urgent and inpatient capacity is required. This is due to the variation in the process; on certain days 100 % of capacity is required to satisfy elective patient demand, thus leaving no room for any other patients. Furthermore, since 17 slots are dedicated to urgent and inpatients, only 83 slots are available for elective patients, which means that ρ is again equal to 1, resulting in an uncontrollable waiting list.

In the case where part of capacity is used for urgent and inpatients, the mean access time can be calculated using a non-preemptive priority $M/M/1$ model [2]. In this model urgent and inpatients are given priority over elective patients, but elective patient treatment is finished once it has started (the non-preemptive property).

Let λ_e represent elective patient demand, λ_u urgent patient demand and λ_i inpatient demand. Assume that urgent and inpatients, if present, are served immediately when treatment of an elective patient is completed. Then,

$$\rho_e = \frac{\lambda_e}{\mu}$$

$$\rho_{u,i} = \frac{\lambda_u + \lambda_i}{\mu}$$

$$\rho = \rho_e + \rho_{u,i}, \tag{4.7}$$

where ρ_e and $\rho_{u,i}$ is the fraction of time the resource spends on elective, urgent and inpatients resp. and ρ is the occupation for the entire facility. The mean access time for elective, $\mathbb{E}[W_e^q]$, resp. urgent and inpatients, $\mathbb{E}[W_{u,i}^q]$, is given by:

$$\mathbb{E}[W_e^q] = \frac{\frac{\rho}{\mu}}{(1-\rho)(1-\rho_{u,i})}$$

$$\mathbb{E}[W_{u,i}^q] = \frac{\frac{\rho}{\mu}}{(1-\rho_{u,i})}.$$

$$\tag{4.8}$$

4.3 Practical Issues

In this section several practical issues related to access time and waiting list management are discussed.

4.3.1 Extremely Long Waiting Lists

If a facility has an extremely long waiting list, an intervention is required before a suitable appointment system can be designed. First it is important to check whether the waiting list is increasing or is more or less stable. If the waiting list is long and still growing, there is an urgent lack of capacity. Next to calculating the required capacity, it should then also be studied whether available capacity can be used more efficiently. Also, temporary additional capacity should be deployed to decrease the size of the waiting list. If the waiting list is stable, it can be concluded that the available capacity is sufficient. However, somehow a backlog of patients evolved over time. In this case additional capacity should be temporarily added to minimize the backlog. Furthermore, the causes of the backlog should be studied, in order to avoid this type of congestion in the future.

4.3.2 Long Waiting Lists and Decrease in Demand

Quite often a long waiting list results in a decrease in demand, especially in densely populated areas where patients can choose between various healthcare providers. The positive side of this is that a natural way of waiting list management occurs. However, from a marketing perspective losing patients to other providers is an undesired side effect. A related effect is that facilities who just minimized their waiting list find themselves in a situation with fast increasing patient demand, insufficient capacity and again, an increasing waiting list. It is very hard to influence these phenomena.

4.3.3 Identification of Patient Groups

Some planners tend to maintain separate waiting lists for each patient group. However, if capacity is shared among these groups, the waiting list should be considered as a whole as well. Allocating capacity per patient group usually results in inflexibility and poor performance, which will be discussed in Chap. 5.

4.3.4 Dealing with Seasonality

Most patient demand is influenced by the time of year. Some patients do not prefer to receive surgery in summer, during winter more people have a cold, if it freezes more people have ice skating accidents and so on. It is impossible to account for all of these influences, but still, if possible the appointment system should be adapted. This means, for example, that if required, more capacity should be offered outside summer and less capacity during the summer holidays. A proper analysis of patient demand and its fluctuations will result in a balanced yearly workload.

References

[1] Cohen JW (1982) The single server queue, 8th edn. North-Holland, Amsterdam
[2] Kleinrock L (1976) Queueing systems: computer applications, vol 2. Wiley, New York
[3] Stanford DA, Renouf EM, McAlister VC (2008) Waiting for liver transplantations in Canada: wait list history 2000–2004 and sensitivity analysis for the future. Health Care Manag Sci 11(2):184–195

Chapter 5
Scheduling Appointment Slots

Using the results provided in the previous chapter, the number of appointments to offer each week can be calculated. This chapter describes how these appointments can be distributed over the week and subsequently over the day.

5.1 Identifying Patient Groups

Usually, patient groups evolve more or less naturally. It is, however, good to reconsider these groups now and then. Natural differentiations usually based on specialty, care provider, urgency, and admission status. Sometimes, a (partial) diagnosis or complaint type is also incorporated, for example in specific consultation hours for hip replacement in Orthopedics or hand surgery in Plastic Surgery. For each patient group that requires dedicated consultation hours which cannot be shared with other patient groups, the number of appointments per week should be determined using formula (4.4). Patient groups which can share capacity can be taken together, subsequently also formula (4.4) can be used to calculate the number of appointments per week for this aggregated group. The next section provides an example of these calculations.

5.2 Introducing Appointment Slots

Specific patient groups require different appointment lengths. This relates to sub-distributions which can be made within a patient group, for example among new and check-up patients. In order to calculate the required appointment time for a patient group, appointment slots are introduced. These slots are blocks of time, equal to or a fraction of the length of all possible consultations. Note that it should be possible to express the length of all possible consultations as a multiple of the chosen slot length.

M.E. Zonderland, *Appointment Planning in Outpatient Clinics*
and Diagnostic Facilities, SpringerBriefs in Health Care Management and Economics,
DOI 10.1007/978-1-4899-7451-8_5, © The Author 2014

Thus, the required weekly capacity, C_I, for a certain patient group, expressed in minutes, equals

$$C_I = \left\lceil \tilde{\mu}_I T \sum_{i \in I} f_i n_i \right\rceil , \qquad (5.1)$$

where f_i is the fraction of subgroup i within patient group I, requiring n_i slots of length T minutes.

Example: Suppose a clinic has two elective Orthopedic patient types: hip and knee patients. An aggregated patient group, consisting of the hip and knee patients, is created, for which the average access time should equal 2 weeks. Since both patient types are either new or check-up patients, there are actually four subgroups:

1. New hip patients, $f_1 = \frac{3}{8}, n_1 = 2$
2. Check-up hip patients, $f_2 = \frac{5}{8}, n_2 = 1$
3. New knee patients, $f_3 = \frac{2}{5}, n_3 = 2$
4. Check-up knee patients, $f_4 = \frac{3}{5}, n_4 = 1$

The slot length $T = 10$ min, and the total appointment demand per week $\lambda = 18$ patients. Since $\tilde{W}_q = 2$ weeks, the number of appointments to offer per week is equal to [recall (4.5)]:

$$\tilde{\mu} = \left\lceil \frac{18 \cdot 2 + \sqrt{(18 \cdot 2)^2 + 4 \cdot 18 \cdot 2}}{2 \cdot 2} \right\rceil = 19. \qquad (5.2)$$

The required weekly capacity in minutes equals:

$$C_I = \left\lceil 19 \cdot 10 (2(\frac{3}{18} + \frac{4}{18}) + 1(\frac{5}{18} + \frac{6}{18})) \right\rceil = 264. \qquad (5.3)$$

Subsequently, the weekly capacity should be divided over the days of operation of the clinic. When doing this, be aware of other processes using the same resource; it is not a good idea to have all doctors working at an outpatient clinic at the same day, since this will result in a high load for both administrative and infrastructural resources.

5.3 Allocation of Slots to Specific Patient Groups

Sometimes it is required to allocate slots to specific patient groups. In this case arrangements regarding the usage of this capacity can be made. For example, appointment slots within this week, which are allocated to semi-urgent patients but not claimed yet, can be filled with elective patients. Urgent slots allocated to-day, but not claimed yet can be filled with inpatients and so on. If it is necessary to allocate appointment slots to specific patient types (for example, because it is medically required), plan these blocks in the middle of the day and plan patients in consecutive order, so that unused capacity can be incorporated in regular capacity again.

Chapter 6
Specific Appointment Systems

In this chapter three specific appointment systems are briefly discussed, which may be of interest for outpatient clinics with certain characteristics.

6.1 Walk-In

In a walk-in system, patients are seen without an appointment. They can literally just "walk in" at the outpatient clinic or diagnostic facility. The main advantage of walk-in systems is that access time is reduced to zero. Furthermore, patients have more freedom to choose the date and time of their hospital visit. However, due to the usually inhomogeneous patient arrival patterns, long waiting times can emerge, together with low utilization of the facility at other points in time. In regular appointment systems workload can be dispersed, although appointment planning is usually time consuming. A walk-in system is most suitable for clinics with short service times and multiple care providers, such as blood withdrawal facilities and pre-anesthesia check-ups for non-complex patients. If the service times are longer or the number of care providers is limited, the probability that patients experience a long waiting time becomes too high, and a regular appointment system would be justified; consider, for example, a Radiology department with two MRI scanners and an average scan time of 30–45 min. With four patients already waiting, the waiting time for a new patient is at least 1 h.

6.1.1 Combining Walk-In and Appointments

Sometimes it is impossible to provide walk-in service for all patients, for example when specific patients need to be prepared for their consultation, or if specific care providers are required, such as anesthesiologists. Also, walk-in patients who experience a full waiting room upon arrival may choose to come back at a later point

M.E. Zonderland, *Appointment Planning in Outpatient Clinics and Diagnostic Facilities*, SpringerBriefs in Health Care Management and Economics, DOI 10.1007/978-1-4899-7451-8_6, © The Author 2014

in time. To make sure that they do have access at that point, clinics usually give these patients an appointment. This combination of walk-in and appointment patients requires a specific appointment system that satisfies the following requirements:

1. The access time for appointment patients is below a certain threshold
2. The waiting time for walk-in patients is below a certain threshold
3. The number of walk-in patients who are sent away due to crowding is minimized

To satisfy these requirements, an appointment system should be developed to determine the optimal scheduling of appointments, not only on a day level but also on a week level. Developing such an appointment system is challenging from a mathematical perspective. The interested reader is referred to [3] for further reference.

6.2 Advanced Access

Advanced access was first described by Dr. Murray [5]. The basic aim of this methodology is to minimize access time ("do today's work today"), by allocating a part of capacity to patients who call in for an appointment the same day or within a few days. The challenge is to determine which part of capacity should be dedicated to these advanced access patients, and which part to patients who require an appointment in the long term. By maximizing the number of patients who are seen within this short time span, access times are minimized. See the articles [2, 4, 6, 7] for further reference.

6.3 Care Pathways

A care pathway is a management tool which helps to organize, usually multidisciplinary, care for patients with identical characteristics, such as disease symptoms, age, and diagnosis. The care pathway specifies all steps in the care process [1] and describes the patient's routing among different care providers and departments. Since the 1990s many healthcare organizations have used care pathways to standardize patient care. Another common goal is reducing the patient's length of stay.

Usually, the appointments for care pathway patients are planned within the department's regular appointment systems. However, in order to achieve the aforementioned short length of stay, usually specific slots are allocated to these patients. The previous chapter has discussed the disadvantages of this working routine in detail. Additionally, prioritizing care pathway patients in an otherwise walk-in clinic may result in long waiting times for walk-in patients (see [8] for further reference).

References

[1] Allen D (2009) From boundary concept to boundary object: the practice and politics of care pathway development. Soc Sci Med 69(3):354–361

[2] Dobson G, Hasija S, Pinker EJ (2011) Reserving capacity for urgent patients in primary care. Prod Oper Manag 20(3):456–473

[3] Kortbeek N, Zonderland ME, Braaksma A, Vliegen IMH, Boucherie RJ, Litvak N, Hans EW (2011) Designing cyclic appointment schedules for outpatient clinics with scheduled and unscheduled patient arrivals. Memorandum 1968, Department of Applied Mathematics, University of Twente, Enschede, The Netherlands

[4] Liu N, Ziya S, Kulkarni VG (2010) Dynamic scheduling of outpatient appointments under patient no-shows and cancellations. Manuf Serv Oper Manag 12(2):347–364

[5] Murray M, Berwick DM (2003) Advanced access: reducing waiting and delays in primary care. J Am Med Assoc 289(8):1035–1040

[6] Qu X, Shi J (2009) Effect of two-level provider capacities on the performance of open access clinics. Health Care Manag Sci 12(1):99–114

[7] Qu X, Rardin RL, Williams JAS, Willis DR (2007) Matching daily healthcare provider capacity to demand in advanced access scheduling systems. Eur J Oper Res 183(2):812–826

[8] Zonderland ME, Boucherie RJ, Al Hanbali AM (2011) Appointments for care pathway patients: the $Geo^x/D/1$ queue with slot reservations. Memorandum 1961, Department of Applied Mathematics, University of Twente, Enschede, The Netherlands

Chapter 7
Improving Clinic Operations

Now all the theoretical foundations for designing appointment systems have been laid, five golden rules for appointment planning are given. Also, management philosophies such as lean manufacturing are briefly addressed. This chapter concludes with an example project, which was carried out at Leiden University Medical Center (a teaching hospital in the Netherlands) in order to reduce workload and patient waiting times at the pre-anesthesia evaluation clinic (PAC).

7.1 Golden Rules for Appointment Planning

In the previous chapters many methods and tools related to appointment planning were discussed. Important insights following from this theoretical foundation are summarized in the following five golden rules for appointment planning.

Golden Rule 1: A Small Buffer Helps to Use Capacity Efficiently, But Do Not Exaggerate. A sometimes used euphemism for waiting time is "appointment buffer." In a way this is true; having a list with spare patients to plan gives flexibility and enables the planner to efficiently use resources. However, this may not be an excuse to maintain reservoirs of patients who will experience extremely long access times. This is patient unfriendly and may result in complications and a longer care trajectory.

Golden Rule 2: Do Not Plan All Incoming Patient Demand Immediately, But Try to Smooth It over the Upcoming Period. Try to find patterns in patient arrivals. Use these patterns to determine required capacity, but try not to overbook patients. Ad hoc creation of extra capacity will result in unused capacity in the future.

Golden Rule 3: Only Use Dedicated Slots If It Is Medically Required. Otherwise, Aim To Be as Flexible as Possible. Dedicated slots result in inflexibility and

M.E. Zonderland, *Appointment Planning in Outpatient Clinics and Diagnostic Facilities*, SpringerBriefs in Health Care Management and Economics, DOI 10.1007/978-1-4899-7451-8_7, © The Author 2014

suboptimal planning. Keep this in mind every time a request for dedicated slots is made (most likely, this will be quite often).

Golden Rule 4: Try to Balance Weekly, Daily, and Hourly Workload. A Small Change in Workload Can Have a Major (Positive or Negative) Effect. Balancing workload is extremely important. Unused capacity cannot be regained, while ad hoc deployment of surplus capacity will in the long term result in an over strained system.

Golden Rule 5: When a New Care Provider Is Appointed, Determine Which Days and Part of the Day Are Most Suitable to Plan Appointments, in Order to Further Balance Workload. In line with the previous rule, this is an easy way to balance workload, since at this stage the new care provider does not yet have an agenda with multiple obligations.

7.2 Management Philosophies

Lately, many processes in healthcare have been intensely studied using management philosophies which originate from industry. An important application area for these philosophies is outpatient clinics and nursing wards. Examples include, but are not limited to: improving administrative processes, reducing patient waiting times, and reducing the amount of required staff. Common used techniques are, for example, lean management, six sigma, theory of constraints, and statistical process control. There are numerous resources available on the Internet discussing the merits of these techniques, therefore they are not discussed in detail in this book. What they do have in common is their aim: the reduction of variance in the process. By making a clear process description and determining (and eliminating) sources of variance, process outcomes such as patient length of stay, waiting and access times can be reduced significantly. However, a drawback of using such well-defined philosophies is that many healthcare organizations forget that most of their problems could also be solved using common sense and simple principles, such as those discussed in the previous paragraph.

7.3 Example Project: Redesign of a Pre-anesthesia Evaluation Clinic

This example is based on [5]. It shows how a relatively simple queuing model is used to improve the operations of a pre-anesthesia evaluation clinic at Leiden University Medical Center in the Netherlands.

7.3.1 The Problem

We consider a PAC. At this clinic, which is operated by the Department of Anesthesiology, patients are screened before elective surgery. In the last decades most hospitals have organized this screening in an outpatient setting. Not only will a well-performed screening reduce the surgical risk for the patient, but also it reduces the number of canceled surgeries due to the physical condition of the patient [3]. Initially, the screening process at the PAC was organized as follows. Four anesthesia care providers performed the actual screening, supported by a secretary and two clinic assistants. The screening consisted of several separate medical and administrative tasks. The majority of patients (70 %) would be screened directly after their consultation at the surgeon's outpatient clinic. This direct (walk-in) screening would only be possible for non-complex patients with ASA I & II classification [1], patients with a more severe health status (ASA III & IV classification) would receive an appointment, since additional medical information and a longer consultation time was required. An increased staff workload, resulting from the introduction of an electronic patient data management system, led to lower job satisfaction, work stress, and prolonged patient waiting times. Although 90 % of the annual 6,000 PAC patients were eligible for walk-in, one third of these patients were seen on appointment basis, due to an overcrowded waiting room when they first presented themselves at the PAC.

7.3.2 The Model

To identify bottlenecks in the PAC's operations, the clinic was modeled as a multi-class open queuing network (see Fig. 7.1). There were three patient classes: children, adults eligible for direct (walk-in) screening, and adults requiring an appointment because of their (more severe) health status. The PAC queuing network has three separate (connected) queues, where the employees act as servers. Patients only enter the PAC through the secretary queue, but may leave the system at any queue. The PAC queuing network was analyzed using a decomposition method, based on the QNA. This method consists of three steps. We first summarize the method and then provide a detailed description of the model with the corresponding formulas.

First, the multi-class network is reduced to a single class network. This is done by aggregating all patient flows that enter a queue. Then the workload ρ is calculated for each queue. This already gives significant and valuable information; recall that ρ is a measure for the fraction of time employees are busy. In the next step, the single class open queuing network is analyzed, where the mean contact time and scv of the joint arrival and service processes at the three queues are deduced. In the final step the mean waiting time per queue is calculated, using the variables that were derived in steps 1 and 2.

In the initial analysis of the PAC queuing network, it was found that the secretary and anesthesia care providers functioned as bottlenecks. Consequently, several

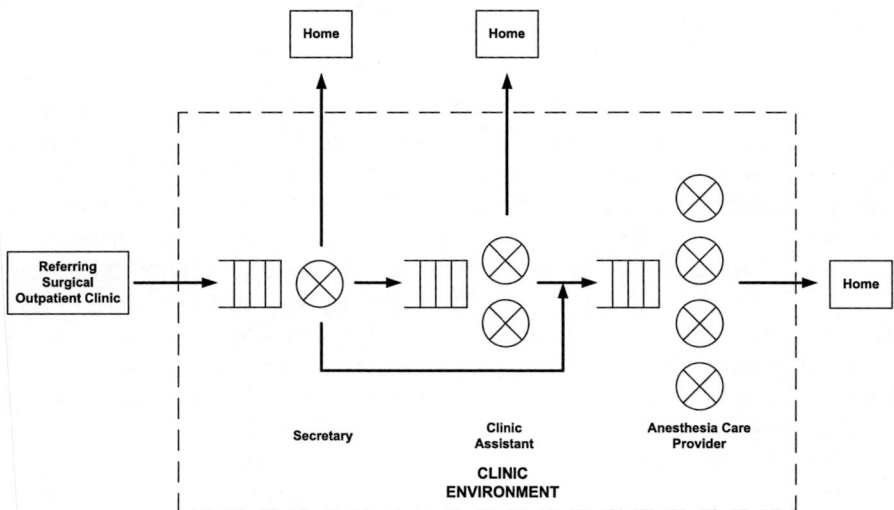

Fig. 7.1 Queuing network representation of PAC

alternatives were formulated together with clinic staff, in order to remove these bottlenecks. All alternatives were evaluated using the queuing network model, resulting in one alternative that outperformed the others. In this alternative, several tasks were redistributed and the patient arrival process was amended such that the arrivals were spread more equally over the day. In the year following the implementation of the alternative clinic design, patient arrivals increased (unexpectedly) by 16 %. In the old situation, this would likely have resulted in even longer patient waiting times (recall Fig. 3.2). However, the mean patient length of stay at the PAC did not increase significantly, and more patients (81 %) were offered the direct screening.

Detailed Description of the Decomposition Method

The PAC queuing network consists of three queues. The secretary queue is a single-server queue whereas the clinic assistant and anesthesia care providers are represented by multi-server queues. Patients enter the queuing network via the secretary queue and depart the system from any of the queues. Furthermore, if upon arrival at a queue an employee is available, patients are served immediately; otherwise, they join the queue and are treated on first come first serve basis. We use an approximate decomposition method [2] that is based on the queuing network analyzer (QNA), developed by Ward Whitt [4], to analyze the model. The model we will present here is more involved than the initial QNA formulation. Practical situations can usually not be directly translated into an existing model. Instead, the theory has to be amended and extended to represent reality. We will describe in detail the changes we have made to the QNA algorithm.

First we introduce some notation. There are k distinct patient classes, where $k = 1$ are patients deferred to an appointment by the secretary, $k = 2$ adults with ASA I or II, $k = 3$ adults with ASA III or IV, and $k = 4$ are children. To evaluate the alternative clinic design, we also introduce $k = \{5,6,7\}$ to represent patients (adults with ASA I or II, adults with ASA III or IV, and children, respectively) who return for their appointment. We have j queues, $j = 1,2,3$, representing the secretary, clinic assistant, and anesthesia care provider.

Step 1.
The aggregated arrival rates at queue j are:

$$\lambda_1 = \sum_{k=1+d}^{4+3d} \gamma_k, \quad \lambda_2 = \sum_{k=2}^{3} \gamma_k, \quad \lambda_3 = \sum_{k=2}^{4} (1 - da_k)\gamma_k + d\sum_{k=5}^{7} \gamma_k, \quad (7.1)$$

where γ_k is the arrival rate of patient class k at queue 1, and a_k is the fraction of patients of class k who are deferred to an appointment in the alternative clinic design. Since the indices $k = \{5,6,7\}$ only exist when the alternative clinic design is evaluated, we introduce the binary variable d, which equals 1 if the alternative clinic design is evaluated and 0 otherwise.

Step 2.
The load per patient class per server for queue 1,2, and 3 is:

$$
\begin{aligned}
\phi_{1,k} &= \gamma_k \mathbb{E}[S_{k,1}] \frac{1}{e_1 s_1} & \text{for} \quad &k = \{1+d,\ldots,4+3d\}, \\
\phi_{2,k} &= \gamma_k \mathbb{E}[S_{k,2}] \frac{1}{s_2} & \text{for} \quad &k = \{2,3\}, \\
\phi_{3,k} &= \gamma_k \mathbb{E}[S_{k,3}] \frac{1}{e_3 s_3} + d(1-a_k)\gamma_k \mathbb{E}[S_{k,3}] \frac{1}{e_3 s_3} & \text{for} \quad &k = \{2,\ldots,4+3d\},
\end{aligned}
$$
$$(7.2)$$

where $\mathbb{E}[S_{k,j}]$ is the mean service time for patient class k at queue j. Since the secretary is often consulted by other patients and coworkers while handling a patient at the reception desk, an effective capacity e_1, $0 < e_1 \leq 1$, is taken into account when calculating the mean time a patient spends at this queue. The anesthesia care provider is often disturbed, but not while treating patients and therefore the effective capacity, e_3, $0 < e_3 \leq 1$, is only used in calculating the load. These effective capacities are calculated by using direct observations and interviews with the employees. The number of servers (i.e., employees) at queue j equals s_j. Adding the load over all patient classes gives the aggregated load per server of queue j, $j = 1,2,3$:

$$\phi_1 = \sum_{k=1+d}^{4+3d} \phi_{1,k}, \quad \phi_2 = \sum_{k=2}^{3} \phi_{2,k}, \quad \phi_3 = \sum_{k=2}^{4+3d} \phi_{3,k}. \quad (7.3)$$

For stability it is required that $\phi_j < 1$ for all queues j.

Step 3.
The flow from queue 1 to queue 2 or 3 and from queue 2 to queue 3 is given by:

$$\lambda_{1,2} = \sum_{k=2}^{3} \frac{(1-da_k)\gamma_k}{\lambda_1}, \quad \lambda_{1,3} = \frac{\sum_{k=4}^{4+3d}(1-da_k)\gamma_k}{\lambda_1}, \quad \lambda_{2,3} = \sum_{k=2}^{3} \frac{(1-da_k)\gamma_k}{\lambda_2}$$

$$(7.4)$$

The fraction of arrivals at queue 3 that come from queue 1 or 2 is given by (note that $q_{1,2} = 1$):

$$q_{1,3} = \frac{\sum_{k=4}^{4+3d}(1-da_k)\gamma_4}{\lambda_3}, \quad q_{2,3} = \sum_{k=2}^{3} \frac{(1-da_k)\gamma_k}{\lambda_3}. \qquad (7.5)$$

Step 4.
The arrival process at queue 1 has scv, $c_{A,1}^2$:

$$c_{A,1}^2 = w_1 \sum_{k=1+d}^{4+3d} Q_{k,1} c_{A,k,1}^2 + 1 - w_1, \qquad (7.6)$$

where $c_{A,k,1}^2$ is the scv of the arrival process of patient class k at queue 1, and

$$w_1 = \left(1 + 4(1-\phi_1)^2(\eta_1 - 1)\right)^{-1}, \quad \eta_1 = \frac{\lambda_1^2}{\sum_{k=1+d}^{4+3d} \gamma_k^2}, \quad Q_{k,1} = \frac{\gamma_k}{\lambda_1}. \qquad (7.7)$$

The mean service time, $\mathbb{E}[S_1]$ and scv at queue 1, $c_{S,1}^2$, are:

$$\mathbb{E}[S_1] = \frac{\sum_{k=1+d}^{4+3d} \gamma_k \mathbb{E}[S_{k,1}]}{\lambda_1}, \quad c_{S,1}^2 = \frac{\sum_{k=1+d}^{4+3d} \gamma_k \mathbb{E}^2[S_{k,1}](c_{S,k,1}^2 + 1)}{\lambda_1 \mathbb{E}^2[S_1]} - 1, \quad (7.8)$$

where $c_{S,k,j}^2$ is the scv of the service time for patient class k at queue j. The arrival process at queue 2 has scv, $c_{A,2}^2$:

$$c_{A,2}^2 = \lambda_{1,2} c_{D,1}^2 + 1 - \lambda_{1,2}, \qquad (7.9)$$

where $c_{D,1}^2$ is the scv of the departure process at queue 1. Queue 2 has mean service time, $\mathbb{E}[S_2]$, and scv, $c_{S,2}^2$:

$$\mathbb{E}[S_2] = \frac{\sum_{k=2}^{3} \gamma_k \mathbb{E}[S_{k,2}]}{\lambda_2}, \quad c_{S,2}^2 = \frac{\sum_{k=2}^{3} \gamma_k \mathbb{E}^2[S_{k,2}](c_{S,k,2}^2 + 1)}{\lambda_2 \mathbb{E}^2[S_2]} - 1. \quad (7.10)$$

The arrival process at queue 3 has scv, $c_{A,3}^2$:

$$c_{A,3}^2 = w_3(q_{2,3}c_{2,3}^2 + q_{1,3}c_{1,3}^2) + 1 - w_3, \quad \text{with}$$

$$w_3 = \left(1 + 4(1 - \phi_3)^2(\eta_3 - 1)\right)^{-1}, \quad \eta_3 = \left(q_{2,3}^2 + q_{1,3}^2\right)^{-1},$$

$$c_{1,3}^2 = \lambda_{1,3}c_{D,1}^2 + 1 - \lambda_{1,3}, \quad c_{2,3}^2 = (1 - d)c_{D,2}^2 + d(\lambda_{2,3}c_{D,2}^2 + 1 - \lambda_{2,3}),$$

$$c_{D,2}^2 = 1 + (1 - \phi_2^2)(c_{A,2}^2 - 1) + \frac{\phi_2^2}{\sqrt{s_2}}(c_{S,2}^2 - 1), \tag{7.11}$$

where $c_{2,3}^2$ is the scv of the patient flow from queue 2 to queue 3, $c_{1,3}^2$ the scv of the patient flow from queue 1 to queue 3, and $c_{D,2}^2$ is the scv of the departure process at queue 2. Queue 3 has mean service time, $\mathbb{E}[S_3]$, and scv, $c_{S,3}^2$:

$$\mathbb{E}[S_3] = \frac{\sum_{k=2}^4 (1 - da_k)\gamma_k \mathbb{E}[S_{k,3}]}{\lambda_3} + d\sum_{k=5}^7 \gamma_k \mathbb{E}[S_{k,3}],$$

$$c_{S,3}^2 = \frac{\sum_{k=2}^4 (1 - da_k)\gamma_k \mathbb{E}^2[S_{k,3}](c_{S,k,3}^2 + 1) + \sum_{k=5}^7 \gamma_k \mathbb{E}^2[S_{k,3}](c_{S,k,3}^2 + 1)}{\lambda_3 \mathbb{E}^2[S_3]} - 1. \tag{7.12}$$

Step 5.
We are interested in the waiting times for patients per queue and the load per employee at each queue. The latter is given by the aggregated load derived in step 1, while the mean waiting times are obtained by using the scv and mean service time calculated in step 2. The mean waiting time, $\mathbb{E}[W_j^q]$, is equal for all patient classes.

$$\mathbb{E}[W_1^q] = \frac{c_{A,1}^2 + c_{S,1}^2}{2} \frac{\phi_1}{1 - \phi_1} \frac{\mathbb{E}[S_1]}{e_1},$$

$$\mathbb{E}[W_j^q] = \frac{c_{A,j}^2 + c_{S,j}^2}{2} \mathbb{E}[W_{j(M/M/s)}^q], \quad \text{where}$$

$$\mathbb{E}[W_{j(M/M/s)}^q] = G_j^{-1} \frac{(s_j\phi_j)^{s_j}}{s_j!} \frac{\mathbb{E}[S_j]}{s_j(1 - \phi_j)^2},$$

$$G_j = \sum_{n=0}^{s_j-1} \frac{(s_j\phi_j)^n}{n!} + \frac{(s_j\phi_j)^{s_j}}{(1 - \phi_j)s_j!} \quad \text{for} \quad j = 2, 3. \tag{7.13}$$

Patient length of stay for each patient class can now be calculated by adding the mean waiting and length of stay of all queues the patient calls at on his/her visit to the PAC.

References

[1] American Society of Anesthesiologists (2011) ASA Score. `www.asahq.org/For-Members/Clinical-Information/ASA-Physical-Status-Classification-System.aspx`. Retrieved 20 April 2011

[2] Bitran GR, Morabito R (1996) Survey open queueing networks: optimization and performance evaluation models for discrete manufacturing systems. Prod Oper Manag 5(2):163–193

[3] Ferschl MB, Tung A, Sweitzer B, Huo D, Glick DB (2005) Preoperative clinic visits reduce operating room cancellations and delays. Anesthesiology 103(4):855–859

[4] Whitt W (1983) The queueing network analyzer. Bell Syst Tech J 62(9):2779–2815

[5] Zonderland ME, Boer F, Boucherie RJ, de Roode A, van Kleef JW (2009) Redesign of a university hospital preanesthesia evaluation clinic: a queuing theory approach. Anesth Analg 109(5):1612–1621

Chapter 8
Challenges in Appointment Planning

Next to the numerous challenges discussed in the previous chapters of this book, three fundamental challenges, which will be increasingly important in the near future and are important with respect to appointment planning, are outlined in this chapter.

8.1 The Healthcare Challenge

Lately, a transition from inpatient to outpatient care has emerged. Medical innovations lead to less invasive treatments, thus a faster recovery of the patient is established. These technical innovations also allow for an increase in possibilities for home care. As a result, the length of stay at nursing wards has decreased dramatically during the last two decades. Next to that, there is a tendency to organize relatively simple procedures in separate, usually commercial clinics. These two developments together will ultimately lead to two types of healthcare providers: clinics where only elective, standardized and profitable care is given, and specialized, high care clinics where urgent, complicated and usually expensive care is provided. Both types of healthcare providers require their own planning methodology, where the development of appointment systems for specialized clinics deserves special attention.

8.2 The Mathematical Modeling Challenge

Usually the development of an appointment system is an activity which is done not very often, at most once a year. Also, most mathematical models which are developed to solve a problem are usually used only once (for example, the queuing model in Sect. 7.3). One of the biggest challenges for operations research professionals is to develop mathematical models which are dynamic in such a way that new, but related problems can be tackled relatively easily, and such that users feel an urge to immediately "grab" the model when a new problem arises.

From a more technical perspective, more research work has to be done in order to optimize appointment planning when several departments are involved (for example, in care pathways), just as in optimal usage of resources which serve multiple patient types (for example, an MRI scanner where urgent patients need to be scanned as soon as possible and elective patients demand a short waiting time).

8.3 The Software Challenge

It is common that hospitals use relatively simple software to plan patients, which is actually nothing more than a digital agenda. It might even be very hard to change the blueprint of the appointment planning or change the length of appointment slots. Planning optimal sequences of appointments or determining the optimal combination of several appointments for one patients on (part of) a single day is often quite difficult, or even impossible. A good appointment planning is supported by a well-developed information system, thus this is a challenge for both hospitals and software developers.

Next to that, the availability of management information is crucial to be in control and to improve processes. The amount of data that is recorded during patient's care trajectories is increasing rapidly. This information should not only be used for administrative purposes, but also to measure process-related outcomes, such as patient's access and waiting time, and resource occupation. This knowledge is the first step to a patient-friendly environment where hospital resources are used efficiently at the same time.